W9-BZO-162

Accelerated Reading

Book Level: 8.0

AR Points: 2.0

Ecosystems of North America

The Rocky Mountains

Larry Bograd

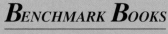

MARSHALL CAVENDISH
NEW YORK

CHANDLER PUBLIC LIBRARY
22 S. DELAWARE ST
CHANDLER, AZ 85225

Thanks to Dr. Dan Wharton, Central Park Wildlife Center, for his careful reading of the manuscript.

Benchmark Books
Marshall Cavendish Corporation
99 White Plains Road
Tarrytown, New York 10591-9001

Copyright © 2001 by Marshall Cavendish Corporation

Illustration by Virge Kask
Map by Carol Matsuyama

All rights reserved

Library of Congress Cataloging-in-Publication Data
Bograd, Larry.
        The Rocky Mountains / Larry Bograd.
            p. cm. — (Ecosystems of North America)
        Includes bibliographical references and index.
        Summary: Examines the different biological communities that exist within the Rocky Mountain ecosystem, describing some of the various plants and animals that are supported by each.
        ISBN 0-7614-0925-4
        1. Mountain ecology—Rocky Mountains—Juvenile literature. [1. Rocky Mountains. 2. Mountain ecology. 3. Ecology.] I. Title. II. Series.
        QH104.5.R6 B64   2000   577.5'3'0978—dc21   99-0455240

Photo Credits
Photo research by Candlepants Incorporated
Cover photo: The Image Bank
The photographs in this book are used by permission and through the courtesy of: Photo Researchers, Inc:
© Jim Steinberg, 4–5, 12–13, 40–41; © Jeff Greenberg, 9, 44; © Alan Carey, 10; © Henry Kyllingstad, 15;
© Francois Gohier, 16 (left); © Charlie Ott, 16 (right); © Pat & Tom Leeson, 17, 19, 26, 27, 33, back cover;
© Adam Jones, 20–21, 48–49; © Dan Guravich, 22; Gale Koschmann Belinky, 24; © Kent & Donna Dannen, 25, 35; © Jess R. Lee, 30–31; © Paula Kohlhaupt/Okapia 1990, 34; © John Mitchell, 36;
© Len Rue, Jr., 37; © Tim Davis, 43; © Anthony Mercieca Photo, 45 (top), 52; © G. C. Kelley, 45 (bottom);
© Phil A. Dotson, 46; © Jeff Lepore, 53; © Pat Caulfield, 54; © Ed Drews, 56–57. The Image Bank: 14.
CORBIS: © Dean Conger, 29; © Kevin R. Morris, 38; © Wolfgang Kaehler, 55. © Bob Winsett, 58. Earth Scenes: © Leonard Lee Rue III, 50.

Printed in Hong Kong
6   5   4   3   2   1

Contents

Top of the World

Whether you are a skier or a snowboarder, a backpacker or a biker, being in the mountains requires a plan. For those in search of the ultimate adventure—reaching one of the highest peaks—the challenge goes beyond bringing along your own food, the latest equipment, and your warmest clothing. You must prepare carefully for everything, especially the unexpected. As some mountain climbers have discovered too late, failure to plan can result in disaster.

In the mountains, the unexpected may take the form of a sudden avalanche sending tons of snow crashing down the mountainside. Or it could be a lightning strike igniting a forest fire that gobbles up countless acres. It might be a flash flood caused by snowmelt, when a tidal wave of water comes roaring through a canyonbed and washes away everything in its path. Because of the expected and unexpected challenges that mountains present, they remain among our last wild—and treacherous—places.

Mountains divide continents and separate countries. They have been cleared of timber and mined for precious minerals, causing hurried mass migrations in a rush to strike it rich. Today, even with skiing and tourism, most of Earth's mountainous territory remains free of human settlement, though not free of our influence.

From snow-capped peaks to lush mountain valleys, few ecosystems sport as wide a range of altitudes as the Rocky Mountains.

Some people assume that nothing can live on mountains because they appear to be so barren. But mountains support an enormous diversity of plant and animal life. The Rocky Mountains offer a unique and varied **ecosystem**, an association of living and nonliving things.

This ecosystem, like others, is defined by the **species**, or kinds, of plants and animals that live here and how they interact with the living and nonliving things, such as the geology and weather, that make up the region. Within the Rocky Mountain ecosystem there are different **biological communities**, species of plants and animals, or **organisms**, that live together and interact at a particular elevation. The place that supplies these organisms with all their survival needs is called their **habitat**.

In 1804, President Thomas Jefferson sent Meriwether Lewis and William Clark to explore the Louisiana Territory and find a land route to the Pacific Ocean. Lewis and Clark crossed the northern Rockies and reached the Pacific in 1805.

The Spine of a Continent

Among the mountains in North America, the Rocky Mountains are dominant. From a human perspective, the Rockies appear as a permanent fixture, but like other geological formations, they are constantly, if very slowly, evolving. The peaks we see today are the products of shifting rock, volcanic activity, and erosion, which have been taking place for more than 70 million years. The deep valleys and rough, craggy slopes are the result of Ice Age glaciers that inched north two million years ago. These glaciers gouged out huge mountain valleys and thousands of small lakes.

The Rocky Mountains are actually a chain of more than sixty mountain ranges, extending 3,000 miles (4,800 km) from Alaska south into northern New Mexico. This immense mountain system bisects North America, dividing east from west. The highest points of the chain create the Continental Divide, or Great Divide. With all of its twists and turns, if the divide were stretched out straight it would measure more than 25,000 miles (40,000 km) long!

Besides establishing a spinelike barrier, the Continental Divide plays a defining role in the continent's water drainage. Rivers on the western side of the divide eventually flow into the Pacific Ocean. Rivers on the eastern side drain into the Atlantic or Arctic Oceans.

The Rocky Mountains

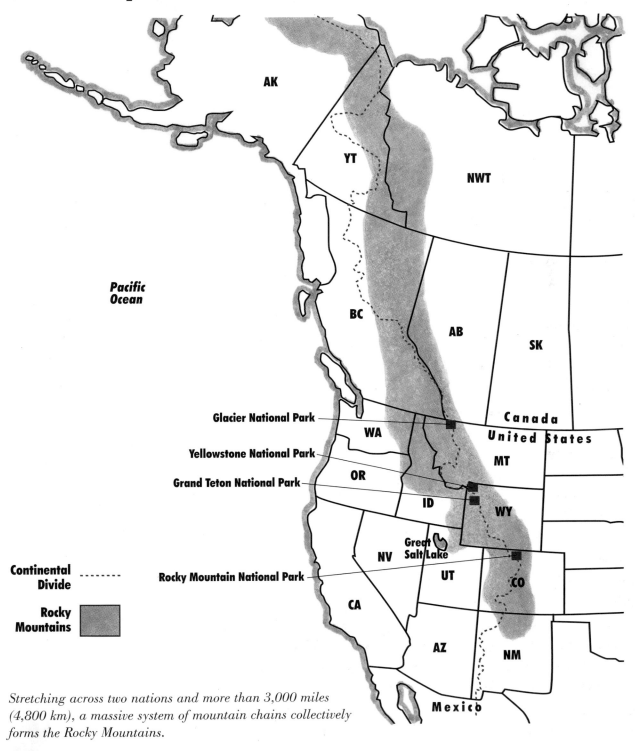

Pacific
Ocean

AK

YT

NWT

BC

AB

SK

Canada

United States

Glacier National Park

Yellowstone National Park

WA

MT

Grand Teton National Park

OR

ID

WY

Rocky Mountain National Park

NV

Great
Salt Lake

UT

CO

CA

AZ

NM

**Continental
Divide** - - - - -

**Rocky
Mountains**

Mexico

*Stretching across two nations and more than 3,000 miles
(4,800 km), a massive system of mountain chains collectively
forms the Rocky Mountains.*

You could stand atop the Continental Divide, empty a bucket of water, and depending on which direction you pour it, send the water toward the Pacific or the Atlantic coast.

Catching Your Breath

Of course, climbing to the top of the Rockies is another matter. One of the defining features of the ecosystem is its "thin" air. Because of the Rockies' high **altitude**, or elevation above sea level, less oxygen is available the higher you climb. Some of the altitudes in the Rockies are very high indeed. In Colorado alone, more than fifty peaks rise at least 14,000 feet (4,267 m) above sea level. To live at such heights, organisms must **adapt**, or adjust, to the thin air. Furthermore, the less dense air allows more **solar radiation**, or energy from the sun, to reach the surface. For people, more solar radiation means an increased risk for sunburn and skin cancer.

At high altitudes, residents must endure a wide range of temperatures. Because the air is so thin, it heats more rapidly than at lower elevations. But the air is unable to trap much of this heat, and so temperatures eventually plummet. For every 1,000-foot (305-m) increase in elevation, the average temperature drops by about 3 degrees Fahrenheit (about 2°C). On some summer days, the temperature on a mountain peak can be 50 degrees Fahrenheit (10°C) cooler than the temperature near the base. Above 9,000 feet (2.7 km), frost is possible any night of the year. In the winter, staying at lower altitudes will not keep hikers any warmer because the mountain valleys are much colder than their surrounding peaks. The dense, frigid winter air sinks into the valleys and collects there.

Rain and snowfall are also greatly influenced by changes in elevation. The prevailing winds in North America travel from west to east. Moisture-rich clouds form over the Pacific Ocean and head east. When they approach the Rocky Mountains, they are forced to rise. As the clouds climb into colder regions, their water vapor condenses, forming rain or snow. So, generally speaking, the higher the elevation in the Rockies, the greater the amount of precipitation it receives.

Altitude also affects the growing season for plants. As elevation increases, there are fewer frost-free nights. In some cases, plants at

Here, you can see two of the mountain's strata, as the altitude plunges from the green strip of conifers to a more aspen-friendly zone.

higher altitudes have less than two months to produce enough seeds and nutrients to survive until the next growing season.

The type of life found in the Rockies depends on which side of a mountain you are observing. North-facing slopes receive less sun than those facing south. As a result, temperatures are lower and moisture levels are higher on north-facing slopes. Because of this, you find organisms, such as the Douglas fir, thriving almost exclusively on these cooler, damper slopes.

Elevation, temperature, available sunlight, moisture, and oxygen are just a few of the factors Rocky Mountain communities must contend with. But despite the challenges, this world of ever-changing conditions, from dizzying heights to deep valleys, makes life impressively diverse.

A Home with a View

Although mountains seem permanent, like ecosystems everywhere, the Rockies are constantly changing. Old plants die or are destroyed

The Rockies include the habitat of the saw-whet owl. It gets its name from its harsh, piercing cry, which some have likened to the sound of a saw being sharpened.

by drought, frost, or fire. New plants take their place. Animals pass through on their migration routes. During this time, the forces of wind and water erode the face of the mountain chains.

The mountains' most defining element, elevation, is all about change. Ask any hiker who has just scaled a slippery slope and has stopped to catch her breath. Rises or dips in elevation mean the terrain is always changing, and this constant flux shapes the kind of communities that live along the mountainside. **Stratification** is the way mountains can be divided into different layers. Different communities can be found at each **stratum**, or level, of elevation. You can enter an entirely new community simply by moving up or down a mountainside.

Each chapter in this book will focus on a specific mountain community in one of our national parks or wilderness areas. More than one hundred years ago, the United States Congress preserved certain regions of the American West. In 1872, the first area set apart "for the preservation, from injury or spoilation, of all timber, mineral deposits, natural curiosities, or wonders . . . and their retention in their natural condition" was Yellowstone National Park in northwest Wyoming and parts of Idaho and Montana. Others followed—Grand Teton National Park (also in northwest Wyoming), Montana's Glacier National Park, and our first stop Colorado's Rocky Mountain National Park.

Stratification

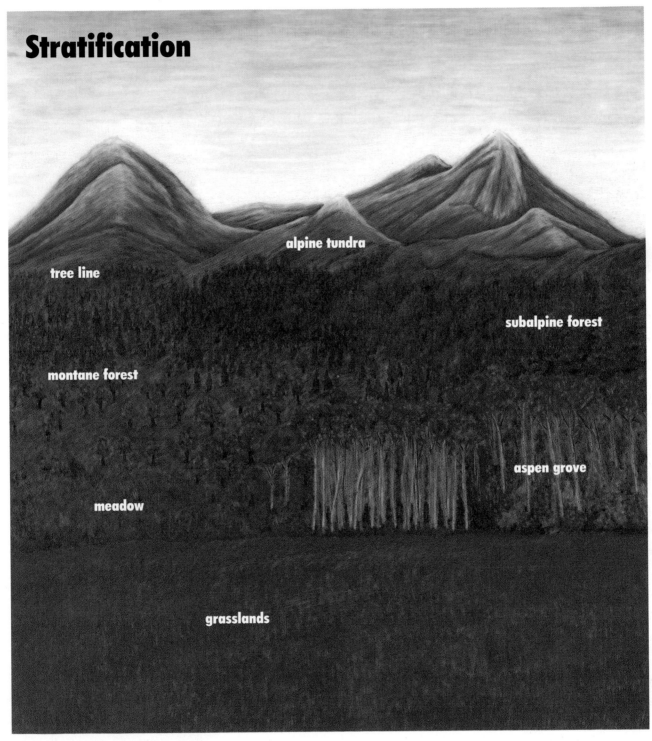

Temperature and precipitation help create a range of habitats at varying altitudes and on opposite sides of the mountains.

Clinging to Life

*O*ne of the most popular roads in North America, used by millions of people, is open only a few months of the year, in the summer and early fall. It is Trail Ridge Road in Rocky Mountain National Park, situated between the Colorado towns of Estes Park and Grand Lake. Because of its high elevation, this famous road receives so much snow that plows do not attempt to clear it until late May.

In our tour of the Rocky Mountains, we will start by taking the Trail Ridge Road to the community at the top of the ecosystem, the **alpine tundra**. Tundra comes from a Russian word meaning "land without trees." The bleak stretches of alpine tundra are among the highest places on Earth, some 11,500 feet (3,505 m) above sea level. Because the air is so thin at this elevation, the alpine tundra is bombarded by intense solar radiation.

Severe weather helps define the tundra. The average annual temperature is below freezing, too cold for trees and many other plants to survive. Such frigid conditions also prevent most cold-blooded animals from surviving here. It can snow any day of the year, and icy blasts of wind whip across the barren land.

Long's Peak in Rocky Mountain National Park is scattered with countless stones.

Instruments have clocked these winds at more than 200 miles per hour (320 km/h)—twice as powerful as the average hurricane. In short, the tundra is a challenging place to call home.

Sparse and harsh, the alpine tundra draws only nature's hardiest specimens.

You Mean Things Can Live Here?

Alpine tundra is the world's highest and one of its harshest habitats. But that doesn't mean it can't support a diversity of life. Particularly during its all-too-brief summers, the tundra is host to a wealth of both permanent and migratory organisms.

The key **adaptation** that allows any organism to survive here is the ability to conserve water and energy. One way to do this is to stay small. Small plants need less food and less moisture to stay alive. Another way, which is specific to plants, is not to reproduce every year. Therefore, almost all tundra plants are **perennials**, meaning they live more than just a single season. Most hug the ground and grow in tight clumps for protection from the wind and cold. They are held in place by large underground root systems. In fact, in some plant communities, the roots make up as much as 90 percent of the entire plant. This is an adaptation that ensures the plant can store enough nutrients to survive the long, cold winters.

Tundra plants do only what is essential for their survival. In a given year, they may grow only a few tiny leaves. They need enough leaves to gather sunlight so they can produce their own food through **photosynthesis**. But too many leaves make them vulnerable to moisture loss and the bitter cold. Many tundra plants are **succulents**. Like desert plants, they can store water in their waxy leaves, whose surfaces help to prevent evaporation.

Despite the scraggly patches of dwarfed vegetation, the tundra is not a bare, dull place. In the summer, the ground explodes with wildflowers. There are yellow alpine avens, actinea, and rydbergia. Dotting the meadows are purple skypilots, blue harebells, alpine forget-me-nots, and the purple of moss campion flowers.

In addition to their short stems and small petals, these flowers sport another essential adaptation. Brightly colored flowers attract flying insects that pollinate the plants, aiding in their reproduction. Fragile, yet incredibly

Also called Scottish bluebell, the slender stems of the harebell grow in clumps and reach a height of 1 to 2 feet (30 to 60 cm).

hardy, tundra plants are living proof that organisms can thrive despite the odds against their survival.

Alpine Zoo

Animals, too, must adapt to the tundra's unique conditions if they are to survive. Only a few animals live here year-round, and they tend to be small, like their short-leafed counterparts. The larger animals that live here, such as the bighorn sheep, are able to cover wide distances in search of food. They are aided by the fact that there are no permanent **predators**, meat eaters, residing on the tundra. There is simply not enough **prey** for these carnivores to survive.

One bird that is a year-round resident is the ptarmigan. This small grouse is well adapted to the habitat with its most important feature, its feathers. Not only do they cover its legs and feet for added

Surefooted, the bighorn sheep can navigate the sheer cliffs of the Rockies, thriving in seemingly unreachable places.

White on white, the ptarmigan's winter feathers make for a perfect match with the snow.

In the warmer months, the pika works furiously, gathering and storing enough food to last the long winter.

warmth, but the bird's plumage changes color to match the season. Its summer feathers are bright layers of black, brown, and white, allowing it to blend in with the moss-covered rocks and boulders. In the winter, the bird is stark white, so it is easily camouflaged in the snow. The ptarmigan has developed a strange habit to deal with the brutal, arcticlike weather. It has been known to wait out severe storms buried inside a snowbank.

Common among the small tundra mammals are the pika and the northern pocket gopher. The pika, a tiny relative of the rabbit, lives in rock fields and feeds in patches of grass nearby. Looking more like guinea pigs than rabbits, pikas seek the safety of colonies, always ready to alert one another of any approaching danger with a high-pitched squeak.

Another mammal, the northern pocket gopher, digs extensive tunnels that undermine the tundra's root system. Rarely seen above ground, these gophers leave mounds of soil scattered across the tundra, the byproduct of their burrowing. Their name comes from their fur-lined cheek pockets in which they carry food. Another adaptation is their lips, which close behind their incisor teeth so they do not get dirt in their mouths when they dig. The gophers are very orderly, reserving certain tunnels for food, others for sleep, and still others for their solid wastes.

The gophers are a mixed blessing to their habitat. They cause a great deal of damage to the habitat with their tunnels. At the same time, they improve and soften the soil by mixing organic matter into the dirt. Their abandoned tunnels provide homes for mice, voles, insects, and other animals. No creature can live in an ecosystem without impacting it in some way.

Larger mammals, such as mule deer and elk, migrate to the tundra in the summer to graze on the thick vegetation. Coyotes, bobcats, jackrabbits, hares, chipmunks, weasels, and foxes join them. Insects are common, but because of the climate, their larvae sometimes take two years or more to mature.

On the tundra, as in other ecosystems, plants and animals depend on one another for survival. They are linked in a series of **food chains** in which certain organisms are eaten by others. The tundra plants at the bottom of the food chains take what nutrients they can from the thin soil. Insects, birds, and mammals eat the plants. In turn, many of these organisms are eaten by predators or die from disease and decompose back into the soil, often with the help of other scavenging insects, birds, and mammals. The decomposed matter enriches the soil, which ultimately enriches the plants. And so, the cycle begins again.

In another tundra food chain, gophers eat roots and insect larvae. The gophers, in turn, are eaten by coyotes or red foxes. A third food chain starts with willow buds, a winter staple of the ptarmigan. The

Like other hibernators, the yellow-bellied marmot spends the summer eating. By the time the animal beds down in September, it has stored up to 60 percent of its body weight as fat to sustain itself until its hibernation ends in May.

ptarmigan, in turn, may be eaten by weasels or bobcats. Plants or meat, predator or prey, each member of the ecosystem has its own unique feeding habits. The interaction among all of these food chains forms a large network of feeding relationships called a **food web**.

The adaptable red fox has a wide range, inhabiting most of the continent north of Mexico.

Full of Life

Although remote, the tundra is visited by tourists often. In the summers, domestic sheep are led here to graze. The damage can be extensive as hikers, vehicles, and these grazing animals destroy the vulnerable vegetation. In a region where the weather stunts normal growth, some plants can take twenty years to return. If heavily disrupted, some areas may need centuries to recover.

Because of this, if you visit Colorado and Trail Ridge Road, hike only the marked trails. Respect the tundra as one of the world's most interesting, yet fragile, biological communities.

winds, let's move down into the next community we are going to study, the subalpine forest of Grand Teton National Park.

Shelter, At Last!

Although we are at an elevation lower than the harsh heights of the tundra, we are entering a community still challenged by altitude and the elements. Subalpine forests are colder, windier, and drier than the communities below them on the mountainside.

Between the dramatic crags of the Tetons, Ice Age glaciers left a series of deep canyons. One is Death Canyon. The trail through this canyon takes us on a six-hour hike, leading us past glacier-carved Phelps Lake, and up into the canyon, where we will spend time in a subalpine forest.

Besides the shelter of tall, narrow-crowned fir and spruce, you might notice that the subalpine forest feels different from other Rocky Mountain habitats. It is relatively humid and cool, even in the summer. This is due to the dense growth of Englemann spruce, subalpine fir, bristlecone pines, and corkbark fir. These trees are among the few able to grow at elevations from 9,000 feet (2,743 m) above sea level up to the tree line. They are evergreens, so they retain their needles year-round and continue to make food during the cold winter months. The needles are short, thin, and have a waxy coating on their surfaces, important adaptations that help the trees

Life along the krummholz zone. Arctic blasts of wind have produced these lopsided trees.

retain moisture. These trees are also **conifers**, which means they grow cones to protect their seeds from hungry birds and mammals. You can think of cones as a sort of hardened flower, especially adapted to harsh climatic conditions.

It is easy to confuse subalpine fir with Engelmann spruce because they are both tall, skinny evergreens. But fir cones grow in an upright position, while spruce cones hang down. Fir needles are also soft, flat, and rounded at the tip, while spruce needles are stiff, square, and sharp-tipped. Despite their differences, all of these trees are well adapted to their community. In protected areas such as Grand Teton National Park, it is not unusual to find conifers that are more than three hundred years old!

Another feature of the subalpine community is its **succession** of trees, the process through which different species of trees thrive and dominate in a given area. Generally, aspen are the first to move into an area cleared by fire, avalanche, or disease. If aspen seedlings are to survive, they require more sunlight than they would ever receive beneath a dense stand of evergreens. So in areas where these coniferous obstacles are removed, aspens are sure to thrive.

In turn, the aspens aid a wide variety of ferns and wildflowers. Dainty blue gentians, cinquefoil, and saxifrage move in, taking advantage of the aspens' patchy shade and the increased sunlight reaching the forest floor. Although aspens may be the dominant species during certain periods of succession, they help create ideal conditions for countless other organisms. In the subalpine forest, nothing stands alone, and nothing lasts forever, either. It may take a century or two, but eventually the aspen will be succeeded by spruce and fir trees, whose taller heights keep sun from reaching the older, shorter aspen. After another hundred years, the aspen disappear completely. The demise of these trees seals the fate of some plants in the understory, which can no longer survive in the heavy shade. However, the aspen roots remain beneath the surface, awaiting the next time the area is cleared so they can sprout again.

Despite this range of trees, the subalpine forest does not have the **biodiversity**, or variety of species, of the biological communities at lower levels on the mountainside. Much like the tundra with its

The Engelmann spruce is a triangular tree with thin, scaly bark.

Forest fire races through a grove of ponderosa pine. Although it seems like a scene of destruction, this fire actually spurs the next generation of growth.

heavy snow, long winters, and short growing seasons, few animal species can survive here year-round. Those that do tend to be warm-blooded and small, such as pine squirrels and snowshoe hares. Tiny deer mice scurry and hide among the numerous fallen and rotting logs on the forest floor. These animals become prey for larger mammals, such as coyotes and red foxes, that venture up the mountain in search of food. One predator, the pine marten, a bushy-tailed weasel-like mammal the size of a house cat, is found only in this habitat. The pine marten is so named because it climbs trees in search of smaller mammals.

Adult black bears range from 5 to 6 feet (1.5 to 1.8 m) in length and weigh 200 to 600 pounds (90 to 270 kg).

Other predators, such as the wolverine and Canada lynx, can be found only in the northern regions of the Rocky Mountains' subalpine forests. They are now extremely rare in lower regions, such as Wyoming and Colorado, where they were once trapped for their fur.

Larger mammals, such as elk and black bears, also pass through the subalpine forests. The elk come here in the summer to graze in the meadows. Bears stay year-round and spend the long winter hibernating.

Like the trees, these animals have adapted to their environment. The snowshoe hare is named for its large, flat feet, which act like natural snowshoes and make for quick escapes, leaving its pursuers bogged down in the heavy snow. The snowshoe hare, as well as the long-tailed weasel, change colors throughout the year, just like

After an absence of more than twenty-five years, the Canada lynx is being reintroduced to the Colorado forest by the state wildlife bureau, which hopes the species will once again prowl this habitat.

Despite the snowshoe hare's white winter coat, the Canada lynx is a crafty hunter, flushing the hare from its hiding spot.

the ptarmigan. Both are brown in the summer to blend in with the forest floor and then turn white in winter to camouflage themselves from predators.

With so many trees, birds abound here, surviving on seeds and insects. Among the most common are hermit thrushes, gray jays, pine siskins, Clark's nutcrackers, mountain chickadees, ruby-crowned kinglets, red crossbills, pine grosbeaks, and woodpeckers. At night, the rare boreal owl might be spotted as it preys upon small mammals.

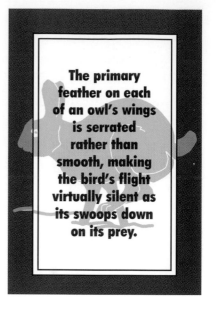

The primary feather on each of an owl's wings is serrated rather than smooth, making the bird's flight virtually silent as its swoops down on its prey.

Nothing Lasts Forever

Even in a community as seemingly unaffected by time as the Grand Teton subalpine forest, change is not only ongoing, it comes in many forms. For example, Engelmann spruce are vulnerable to a number of insect invaders. The most notorious is the Engelmann spruce beetle, which has wiped out entire stands of the tree. The western spruce budworm prefers spruce and fir. Not really a worm, the budworm is a highly destructive, leaf-eating caterpillar. Elk enjoy nibbling on young trees as well. All of these organisms alter the complexion of the landscape, aiding succession as they eat their fill. When tiny insects bore into these towering trees, they are helping to make way for the next wave of dominant trees.

Lightning and **windfall**, the destruction caused by violent storms, can also harm large growths. Yet, as elsewhere, the slow, natural cycle of succession is altered by the greatest threat to this community—humans. Until the 1950s, the subalpine forests were seldom logged. But as forests in more settled areas were cleared, loggers looked to the subalpine forest. Entire mountainsides have also been cleared or partially cleared for ski areas. The biggest threat, however, comes from forest fires sparked by people. Although fires are surprisingly healthy for the forest, clearing out old growth and opening new spaces, it still takes the forest years to recover.

What is lost when trees are removed is critically important. These trees hold an immense amount of snow throughout the winter.

A logger cuts a wedge into a tree to direct its fall.

When the snow melts, it feeds rivers and reservoirs that are the sources of much of our drinking and agricultural water.

If a tree falls in a forest, does it make a sound even if no one is there to hear it? Of course. It sounds a warning for our wise management of this magnificent subalpine community.

Stiff Competition

As we make our way down from the mountaintop, the air becomes easier to breathe, the weather less harsh, and the communities grow more complex. Let's stop at the community beyond which most weekend hikers rarely venture, the **montane forest**. This community forms a broad band around the sides of mountains, sandwiched between the subalpine forests above and the shrubby vegetation, valleys, grasslands, and meadows below.

We are between 5,500 and 9,000 feet (1.7 and 2.7 km), the elevation of most ski areas, mountain resorts, and vacation cabins. Here, too, many of the boom-and-bust mining camps sprang up in the nineteenth century, as prospectors endured terrible living conditions in the hopes of striking it rich.

One of the most famous places in the Rocky Mountains is Yellowstone National Park, the nation's oldest national park, occupying northwest Wyoming and neighboring parts of Idaho and Montana. We will explore Yellowstone's montane forest, a rich stratum that is the site of some intense **competition** among the many organisms that make their homes here. Because the climate is so much more hospitable, there is greater

Yellowstone National Park is a name synonymous with the American Rockies.

biodiversity on this strip of the mountains. The montane forest is a crossroads of Rocky Mountains organisms, some permanent residents, some passing through. Few plants and animals are equipped to endure the conditions at higher altitudes, so they occupy this stratum, competing with each other for the things they need to survive. Although the montane forest is lusher than the windswept tundra and offers a larger amount of food, there is only so much to go around. Here, only the strongest or the best adapted will thrive.

Trees Fighting Back

As in other mountainous places, Yellowstone's soil is not very rich in nutrients. If a tree cannot get nutrients from the soil, then it has to manufacture more of its food itself. One reason that conifers thrive here is that they keep most of their needles for several years. By doing so, a conifer requires fewer nutrients and less water than deciduous trees, which must grow new leaves each spring.

Have you ever leaned against a pine tree and come away with sticky sap clinging to your skin or clothing? Sap, or **resin**, is another adaptation to this habitat. Sap is like the scab that forms to protect an injury to our skin. This resin is released at points of injury, where the tree was invaded by fungi or insects. It quickly hardens into shiny, golden amber that seals the wound and protects the area from further harm.

In most montane forests, the two dominant trees are ponderosa pine and Douglas fir. Separating to opposite slopes is one way of solving the dilemma of competition and the fight for the best space along the mountainside. Ponderosas grow mostly on lower, south-facing slopes. They are easy to recognize because they have the longest needles—4 to 7 inches (10 to 18 cm)—of any conifers. Douglas firs grow on cooler and wetter north-facing slopes. They are dense, dark-green trees with short needles. Douglas firs are actually more closely related to hemlock than to other firs. The largest Douglas firs in Yellowstone are at the Pine Creek Campground, but you can find them throughout the park.

Other types of trees found here include aspen and lodgepole pine. Yellowstone boasts the largest stands of lodgepole pines in the

Ponderosa pines have thick trunks and are known for their soft, pliable wood.

United States. One of the tree's special adaptations is cones that require intense heat to open. This allows lodgepole pines to quickly populate an area that has been destroyed by fire. The fire loosens the seeds that sprout rapidly in the wide swaths of charred ground. Through this adaptation, the lodgepole pines edge out the other

montane trees in claiming the newly opened space on the forest floor.

No Need for Weeds

We are now at a level where the land starts to flatten out and widen a bit. As a result, we will start to see a lot of wildflowers, grasses, and shrubs. You will find an abundance of wildflowers such as purple lupine, golden banner, and fairy slippers especially among the straight and evenly spaced trunks of lodgepole pines. Not only does the slope accommodate more diverse plants, but the weather is less extreme, too. Summers are long, hot, and fairly dry. Winters are cold, but hardly as brutal as at higher elevations. Many plants thrive here partially because of the ideal weather.

It is because conditions are so favorable here that competition strongly affects the success of montane plants. With wildflowers, competition often occurs in the form of weeds. Weeds usually arrive from outside the

> **Lodgepole pine was so named because Native Americans used its straight form and height to anchor their lodges and tepees. Today, we use this pine for telephone poles and log homes.**

You can identify Russian knapweep by its wiry stems and bristly purple heads.

community, sometimes from another ecosystem. They are introduced in a number of ways: as seeds carried by the wind or in the fur, plumage, or waste of animals passing through the area. Weeds do well precisely because their new home lacks natural enemies to prevent them from spreading. Here in Yellowstone, as elsewhere in the Rocky Mountains, the weeds sometimes assume a variety of disguises. They aren't always as thorny or as ugly as you'd think. On the contrary, many of the flowers you see along trails and roads are actually weeds. Canada thistle, Russian knapweed, dandelions, and even some members of the daisy family are all weeds, and all pose a threat to other plants. These weeds crowd out native plants and often grow taller, forcing the natives to grow in their shadows. Once the weeds have established a foothold, the competition for nutrients and sunlight grows even more intense.

Golden banner announces itself in bursts of yellow dotting the forest floor.

Oh Deer, It's a Bear!

Just as plants are more diverse and more plentiful in the montane forest, so are the animals that live here. The greater the variety of food chains, the larger the number of animals that are drawn into the food web. ·

With its warmer conditions, this is the highest mountain elevation where large reptiles can survive. Toads, frogs, lizards, turtles, and tiger salamanders are typically found below 8,000 feet (2.4 km). Several species of snakes also thrive in this range, among them the bull snake. In order to gain the advantage over the countless other competing montane predators, this snake has developed a unique adaptation. Although the bull snake finds a majority of its prey on the ground, this acrobatic reptile has been known to climb trees in search of birds and small mammals.

These reptiles and amphibians feed on some of the 12,000 species of insects found in this habitat. Beetles, flies, ants, wasps, bees, and butterflies are not only food for reptiles, amphibians, and birds, but they are also responsible for pollinating flowering plants.

Bull snakes typically hunt in pine groves, where they prey on small mammals and ground-nesting birds. Occasionally, they'll climb for a meal.

Other insects help aerate the soil by burrowing tunnels deep into the forest floor. Of course, not all insects help the community. Grasshoppers can strip grasslands as quickly and effectively as elk. Although this digging and chewing appear to be destructive, they are all part of maintaining the health of an ecosystem and aid the forest's natural transitions and cycles of succession.

Among the most popular animals at Yellowstone is the mule deer. This large yet graceful mammal is so named because of its mulelike ears. As an adaptation to a habitat filled with carnivores, such as coyotes, cougars, and wolves, each ear can turn separately to allow the deer to hear distant sounds coming from different directions. Mule deer tend to congregate near the edges of aspen stands. Grasses, low shrubs, and other foods are more plentiful there than in the

Ranging from the desert to the subalpine forest, mule deer can thrive practically anywhere, as long as they have a supply of water and food.

conifer forest, yet the shelter of the evergreens is always nearby. But found throughout the entire Rocky Mountain ecosystem, mule deer are generally always on the move. If competition for choice vegetation becomes too stiff in a given area, these wide-ranging animals simply move on.

What would a trip to Yellowstone be without mentioning its most famous residents, the bears? Two species of bear live here. By far the most common is the black bear, which is not always black. It may be black, brown, or even light brown. A generation ago, black bears literally stopped traffic at the park and were constant visitors to campground garbage cans. However, today park rules are better enforced, and garbage control has improved. As a result, bears are rarely seen

Although adult grizzly bears can weigh up to 900 pounds (410 kg), they are surprisingly agile. Some have been known to run up to 30 miles an hour (48 km/h).

where humans gather. That does not mean they have disappeared. In fact, the bear population has grown so much that they have now spread out onto nearby private land and ranches. Adopting a broader habitat or range is another response to increased competition within a species.

The other Yellowstone bear is the grizzly. Although grizzlies subsist largely on grasses, roots, seeds, berries, and insects, they are still highly dangerous carnivores. Once common in the northern Rockies, the grizzly's numbers have declined to the point that the animal is now on the list of threatened species. These days, it is very rare to spot one at Yellowstone.

No Yellowstone Unturned

Because of its beauty and accessibility, the montane forest has been greatly altered by human presence. Yellowstone is host to more than three million human visitors every year. Yet even with the park's roads, campgrounds, hiking trails, and recreational areas, 98 percent of its 3,400 square miles (2.2 million acres or .89 hectares) remains untouched. Here, visitors can still experience one of the largest and most pristine natural places on Earth.

Key to Survival

In the Elk Mountains, in the heart of the Colorado Rockies, aspens have the distinction of being the dominant deciduous trees. In the aspen forest, they are the only deciduous trees, other than scattered cotton-woods growing in the moist soil of riverbanks and marshes. Like other deciduous trees, aspens lose their leaves as a way to conserve moisture during the winter, when the roots cannot absorb water from the frozen soil. During these frigid months, the trees enter a dormant, or resting, stage.

Autumn here is signaled by leaves turning orange, red, yellow, or brown. In the Rocky Mountains, the aspens announce the approach of winter by turning from pale green to brilliant gold. Aspens are often referred to as "quaking" or "trembling" because their thin leaves twist back and forth in the wind. This is not to suggest, however, that aspens are fragile or weak. Although aspens are vulnerable to harsh weather and disease like any trees, some groves on the western slope of Colorado's Continental Divide are several thousand years old!

The famous ski resort town of Aspen, Colorado, takes its name from this stately tree. Not far from this

Colorado's Elk Mountains rise like an island amidst a sea of aspens in their peak autumn gold.

winter playground are the Elk Mountains. This range is among the most rugged and beautiful in the state. Filled with red slate and sandstone canyons and half a dozen granite "aeries" (mountains taller than 14,000 feet, or 4,267 m), the Elk range contains many of the largest and most spectacular aspen groves in the world.

A Sucker Born Every Year

Strange as it may seem, an entire aspen grove can be just one tree. This is because aspens produce an enormous network of roots. When a root growing underground finds a spot where it can reach sunlight, it sends up a "sucker" that eventually becomes a tree. As more and more suckers grow from its roots, one aspen can cover an entire hillside.

Aspens can achieve tremendous heights. The largest aspen is located in Michigan and measures 109 feet (33 m) tall and more than 120 feet (36 m) wide. Colorado, particularly on the western slope of the Continental Divide, has many aspens of its own that could vie for the title.

When it comes to succession, aspens are among the first species to take over a clearing. This is because the aspens' root system can live for thousands of years, whether it produces trees above ground or not. These roots can lie dormant, waiting for natural or human forces to clear an area for new growth.

This root system is not the only way that aspens ensure future generations. A single tree may produce thousands of seeds, which sport long silky hairs that allow them to catch a gust of wind and sail long distances. Only a few of these seeds will ever sprout, but those that do have a high rate of survival.

Besides its extraordinary root system, another reason for the aspen's success is its ability to grow in different types of soil. It does not matter much to the adaptable aspen whether the soil is wet, dry, rocky, or mostly clay. Once aspens take hold, though, their fallen leaves decompose and enrich the soil. Conifer needles are slow to decompose, but the cycling of nutrients from deciduous trees back into the soil is a relatively quick process. Decaying leaves, in turn, draw insects, which then attract carnivorous birds and small mammals, and on up, all the way to the top of the food chain.

With its distinctive five-petalled flowers, the columbine draws bees and hummingbirds because it holds large amounts of nectar.

With good soil and enough moisture retained by the sheltering trees, flowers are plentiful in the aspen forest, including the Colorado state flower, the columbine. In addition, shrubs abound. The juniper and many members of the berry family, such as the chokecherry, snowberry, and serviceberry, all provide color, shelter, and food for aspen forest inhabitants.

While some species compete for survival, others offer aid, providing shelter and food to a countless array of plants and animals. These "helpful" organisms are known as **keystone species**, and they have a large effect on other members of the community. In the Rocky Mountains, one such species is the aspen.

Random branches and scruffy tufts of leaves mark the quaking aspen. A breeze sets the whole tree in motion.

Aspen groves provide nourishment for a horde of mammals. Elk and mule deer—even an occasional black bear—feed on the buds and leaves in the summer. In winter, elk will eat the bark, particularly when the low-growing plants are covered with snow. Elk migrating through the grove often stop so the females, or cows, can give birth in the protection of the dense shrubs. Moose and beavers enjoy the bark as well. The bark is high in vitamin K, which is necessary for blood clotting. It also contains salicylic acid, an ingredient in numerous products, including aspirin. Native Americans knew of the benefits of aspen bark and used it to treat cuts, broken bones, fevers, rheumatism, and other ailments.

The winged members of this community also benefit greatly from the aspens' presence. Western warbling vireos, bluebirds, and robins find places to nest in the trees, plus plenty of seeds, insects, and nectar-bearing flowers that thrive in the sunny groves. Northern flickers and hairy woodpeckers hollow out nests in the soft aspen trunks. When these birds abandon their

Western warbling vireos prefer to live in forests. They are known for their short, loud songs, which they repeat over and over.

In addition to bark, moose feast on a variety of grasses, herbs, and submerged aquatic plants.

The antlers of a male elk, or bull, tower about 4 feet (1.2 m) above its head. Each horn usually sprouts five smaller tines.

holes, swallows, nuthatches, wrens, and even small owls
are waiting to move in. In this way, the aspen trunk is
like a hotel. After one guest has moved on, another one
is waiting to check in.

The animals you find in an aspen grove are similar
to the residents of the montane forest. They include
small carnivores such as the long-tailed weasel and the
shrew. Pocket gophers fare much better here than higher
up the mountain. They scurry about with their cheeks
stuffed with food. These shy creatures hardly affect the
aspen at all. It is the beaver that poses the greatest
threat to the trees' survival. A beaver can eat nearly
1,500 pounds (680 kg) of aspen in a year.

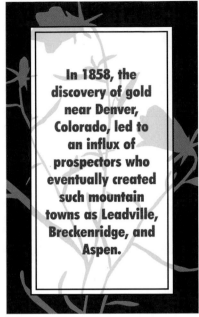

In 1858, the discovery of gold near Denver, Colorado, led to an influx of prospectors who eventually created such mountain towns as Leadville, Breckenridge, and Aspen.

Log Jam

No organism stands alone as it goes about the hard work
of surviving in the aspen forest. Whether it is in the
intricate links of a food chain or the far-reaching influence of a keystone species, each ecosystem is composed of a large network of
interconnections. Here, the aspen stands at the center of a wide web
of organisms dependent on the tree for their survival. So its future
must be ensured.

Beavers are not the only mammals that exploit aspen groves.
Although humans prefer coniferous trees for most commercial purposes,
aspens increasingly are being harvested for their wood. Aspen ends
up in paneling or pressed building products such as particleboard.

Still, it is the aspen's beauty that draws us to it. While the
Douglas fir may define the Canadian Rockies, it is the aspen, more
than any other organism, that defines the Colorado Rocky Mountains
and the famous ski town named in its honor.

Wide and Dry

Glacier National Park, located in northwestern Montana on the border between the United States and Canada, is aptly named. This area was heavily affected by Ice Age glaciers, and you can see remnants of them in the park today. These powerful, incredibly slow-moving glaciers inched north, leaving behind a series of large, U-shaped communities and fjordlike lakes.

After trekking through the higher elevations, it is quite a change to move down to the next stratum, the mountain valley, where the land flattens into meadows. Just as different plants and animals live on the different slopes of a mountain, the species at the mountains' base change, too, depending on whether you are on the eastern or western side of the Continental Divide.

Go West!

To the west of the Great Divide, as we move farther down the mountains of Glacier National Park, we tend to find montane shrubland. It is a bit surprising, after being in thickly forested communities, to come here and be able to see for long distances. It's quite a change as well to find so few trees. In their absence grow a variety of shrubs, most no taller than 3 to 4 feet

Long ago, retreating glaciers scooped out deep valleys and sliced off walls of rock. Today, this place is preserved as Glacier National Park.

(1 to 1.2 meters). This is due, in part, to the arid climate and poor soil. The area is dry because vapor-heavy clouds pass overhead and dump their moisture on higher ground. The soil is loose because of the lack of trees to hold it in place. Water erosion carries off the fertile topsoil, particularly in the spring when the snow thaws and water rushes down the mountainsides in rivulets and streams.

One common mountain valley plant is the scrub oak, which grows in thickets. This plant tends to be small due to the lack of precipitation. But what the scrub oak lacks in size, it more than makes up in color. Its bright orange and red autumn leaves rival the aspen's gold as the most vibrant in the Rockies.

Another keystone species, the scrub oak is like a cafeteria to the animals that feed here, offering something for everyone. Mule deer like the branches and twigs. Rock squirrels and two species of birds, band-tailed pigeons and scrub jays, enjoy the acorns the oak produces. Insects and their larvae live under the bark and inside fallen acorns that are rotting on the forest floor.

Scrub oaks are small shrublike trees that thrive in dry soil.

Design Your Own Spring Runoff

When the spring thaw melts the snow and feeds rivers and streams, it also causes erosion, particularly at higher elevations, where the slopes are steep. This experiment shows the effect of erosion, especially on a steep grade. Do the experiment outside, if possible, so spilled water will not be a problem.

You will need:

- a strong cardboard box
- a plastic garbage bag
- a small bag of sand
- small rocks and/or plastic trees
- a block of wood
- two large plastic buckets: one filled with water and one empty

1. Line the box with the plastic garbage bag.
2. Fill the bottom about half full with sand. Gradually build up the sand toward one end of the box.
3. Arrange rocks and/or the plastic trees.
4. Rest the end of the box that contains the most sand on the block of wood.
5. Place the empty bucket under the low end of the box to catch the runoff.
6. At the high end of the box, drizzle water onto the sand.

As the water moves downhill, it will probably carry part of the slope with it. With enough force, the water may even carry away rocks or trees. Healthy trees, however, have extensive root systems to hold the soil in place and resist erosion. What would happen to the soil if these trees were removed from the forest?

What happens to the rate of erosion in your experiment as you increase the steepness of the slope?

The scrub oak is not the only native plant that produces a lot of nuts, fruit, and seeds. It is joined by skunkbrush, snowberry, service-berry, and mountain mahogany. As a result, the montane shrubland draws many **herbivores**—plant-eating organisms—such as black bears, foxes, skunks, ground squirrels, deer mice, and many birds, including lazuli buntings, wild turkeys, green-tailed towhees, and Virginia's warblers.

With its turquoise head, brown breast, and white undersides, any bird-watcher will tell you, this is a male lazuli bunting.

More often, though, many of the valley's plants have developed defenses to ward off hungry herbivores. The sagebrush has tiny flowers with no petals, clustered in protective spikes—not exactly inviting to hungry animals. Greasewood is a stiff, low-growing shrub that suits the taste of a select few. It is toxic to most animals, yet provides nutrition for black-tailed jackrabbits, mule deer, and pronghorn antelopes.

Go East!

On the eastern side of the Continental Divide, we descend from the montane forest of Glacier National Park directly to the grasslands below. Grasslands are commonly found at lower elevations, although they are also found in large mountain valleys or meadows. At higher elevations, these wide, open areas are called "parks."

Grasslands, like shrublands, are very dry because most precipitation falls at higher elevations as clouds condense over the mountaintops. The dry conditions, combined with very cold winters and year-round exposure to high winds, make this habitat a tough place for plants of any size to survive. Most trees can grow only alongside a river, creek, or lake. The grasslands feature a variety of short grasses, such as

Eventually the mountains and rolling hills level off. The flat plains of grass take over and stretch on for miles.

buffalo grass and blue grama, that send their anchoring roots deep into the soil.

Like the plants adapted to this dry habitat, native animals must cope with the limitations of this community. Many small mammals are so well adapted that they do not need to drink water. Ord's kangaroo rats are one such animal. Their water supply comes exclusively from the plants they eat.

Many other animals spend a lot of their time underground, escaping the worst of summer heat and winter cold. Northern pocket gophers have an enormous impact on this ecosystem with the extensive tunnel systems they dig. They harm some plants, tearing up and eating root systems as they burrow underground. Offsetting the damage, the gophers' tunnelling helps loosen and aerate the soil. Their digging also creates mounds of bare soil above ground, where native and nonnative plants may take root.

Another burrowing native is the prairie dog, which has lived in this habitat for more than 450,000 years! Prairie dogs live in large underground communities, or towns. Some towns are so large that they house thousands of animals. However, in many areas of the West, these towns are being destroyed to build human settlements. While the prairie dogs are not threatened with extinction, their numbers have been severely reduced.

These eastern slope grasslands eventually become part of the Great Plains, another fascinating and distinct ecosystem. Until 150 years ago, few

Prairie dogs often stand watch at the entrances to their burrows. They keep the grass cropped close so they have a clear view of any approaching predators.

humans, except for scattered Native American nations and white trappers and prospectors, lived on the Great Plains. Now, it is almost impossible to find a stretch of the Great Plains not overrun by people.

Many species of mammals, birds, and insects did not survive this human invasion. Larger mammals, such as pronghorns and bison, once filled the grasslands in large numbers. Areas that once sustained these animals are now used for cattle grazing or agricultural activities. Before widespread human settlement, native grasses captured the small amount of rain and protected the fragile soil from wind erosion. In the last century, intensive grazing and other farming practices removed this native grass cover, exposing the soil, which slowly but surely is being blown away or weakened by overuse.

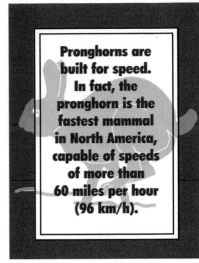

Pronghorns are built for speed. In fact, the pronghorn is the fastest mammal in North America, capable of speeds of more than 60 miles per hour (96 km/h).

As agriculture claims more and more acreage, pasturelands inch closer to the Rockies.

Tomorrow's Rocky Mountains

*L*ike other North American ecosystems, the Rocky Mountains have been greatly affected by the large number of humans either living here or visiting the area as tourists. Yet when you reach the top of a wilderness mountain after a hard but rewarding hike, you might look in all directions and see no signs of human activities. Instead, you see other rugged peaks, mountainside forests, and glacier-fed lakes. For a moment, you feel like an explorer, enjoying the illusion that you are the first human to scale such heights.

Only a few generations ago, this illusion was accurate, but no longer. The mountainous West is among the fastest-growing human settlements on the continent. More and more often, wilderness can be found only in preserved areas, such as our great national parks and national or state forests.

By definition, biological communities are dynamic and always changing. The aspen grove of today will, in a few hundred years, become a fir or spruce forest. Today's marsh may dry up and become tomorrow's meadow. On a slower scale, glaciers and erosion will continue to change the appearance of mountains and canyons. Yet due to human influence, some changes in

Shooting its stream of boiling water more than 100 feet (30 m) in the air, Yellowstone's famous geyser Old Faithful always draws a crowd.

the Earth's ecosystems have accelerated, especially in the last few centuries.

What had been uninterrupted grasslands are now largely claimed for agriculture and grazing, sectioned off by barbed-wire fences, irrigation ditches, or roads. Forests have been altered by logging. Forest fires are set by human carelessness or on purpose, and strip-mining has eaten up vast tracts of wilderness. Entire slopes and mountain valleys have been cleared for ski areas throughout the Rockies. Although acid rain is not the problem it is in the great forests of the central and northeastern United States, it affects even the most remote communities in the West. Acid rain is caused by the emissions that are released into the atmosphere from many industrial sources, including the coal-burning power plants that are generating electricity for a growing human population.

Drop by Drop

How do adverse changes in the Rocky Mountains affect us? As the highest place on the North American continent, this ecosystem is the source of much of the water we need to survive. Places as far away as southern California or eastern Iowa use water that begins as snowmelt high in the Rocky Mountains. Although the highest alpine rivers are still relatively clean, you do not have to go very far down the mountains to find water polluted with pesticides and other toxic chemicals.

Any attempts to remedy the damage must begin with educating ourselves about what is at stake. When we appreciate the wonder and diversity of life in this and other ecosystems, we will be less inclined to allow it to deteriorate.

Every path, every human presence alters the face of the Rocky Mountains. We must balance our fun with prudent management of this geological wonder.

The Effects of Acid Rain

Although acid rain is not the widespread problem in the Rocky Mountains that it is in more industrialized areas, it still remains a real threat to the ecosystem. Enormous coal-burning plants on the western slope of the Continental Divide release harmful chemical emissions into the air. Wind carries them over the mountains, where the emissions mix with water vapor to produce acid rain. This vapor doesn't always fall as rain, though, especially in the mountains, where most of the precipitation arrives as snow.

This experiment allows you to demonstrate the effects of acid rain on plants, using a vinegar solution as the acid rain. Before you start, record what you think the results will be.

You will need:

- eight fast-growing plants, such as radishes or beans, planted in separate pots
- labels for the pots
- a measuring cup
- water
- white vinegar
- an empty jug for mixing solutions
- a journal

Whether you start your plants from seed or transplant them, wait until they are strong and stable.

1. Divide the eight plants into four groups of two. Label two pots Group 1, two pots Group 2, two pots Group 3, and two pots Group 4.
2. Water Group 1 with with about 1 cup tap water.
3. Water Group 2 with a solution of 3 cups (60 ml) vinegar and 3 cups (60 ml) water.
4. Water Group 3 with a solution of 3 cups (60 ml) vinegar and 9 cups (180 ml) water.
5. Water Group 4 with a solution of 3 cups (60 ml) vinegar and 15 cups (300 ml) water.
6. Water each group with the same amount of liquid when the soil feels dry, but be careful not to overwater the plants. Be sure that the growing conditions (sunlight, warmth) are identical for all groups. Rotate the pots to provide equal amounts of sunlight.
7. In your journal, record the growth rate and appearance of the plants every other day for three weeks.

Analyze your results. Were you right? Can plants survive with low levels of acid in the precipitation? What would happen if you put other items—a chicken bone, leaves, a hard-boiled egg, seashells—in the various solutions? What might this tell you about the effects of acid rain on animal life?

Glossary

adapt to adjust.

adaptation the special features and behaviors developed by organisms to maximize their chances of survival and reproduction in a specific location. The large, individually moving ears of the mule deer are an adaptation that allows it to hear the sounds of potential danger near and far.

alpine tundra the treeless area near the tops of high mountains. The tundra discussed in this book can be found in the Rocky Mountain National Park near Trail Ridge Road.

altitude elevation above sea level.

biodiversity the variety of animal and plant species sharing an area.

biological community all of the organisms that live together and interact in a particular environment.

competition the struggle among organisms to get what they need for survival.

conifers evergreen trees that have needles instead of leaves and cones containing seeds.

ecosystem the association of living things in a biological community, plus its interaction with the nonliving parts of the environment.

ecotone the area where two neighboring communities meet.

food chain a feeding relationship in which one organism is eaten by another, which, in turn, is eaten by another.

food web the interaction among all the food chains.

habitat the place that has all the living and nonliving things that an organism needs to survive and reproduce.

herbivore an animal that eats plants. Pikas and prairie dogs are examples of herbivores.

keystone species a species that has a large effect on many species in its community or ecosystem. The aspen is a keystone species because it helps support many other organisms, such as bluebirds, elk, and beavers.

krummholz a German word meaning "crooked wood."

montane forest a cool, upland community occurring between the subalpine forest and shrubby vegetation, characterized by conifers.

organism a living thing, such as a plant or animal.

perennial a plant capable of surviving two or more years without having to reproduce itself by seed every year.

photosynthesis the chemical process by which plants and certain other organisms containing chlorophyll use sunlight, carbon dioxide, and water to make sugars and other substances.

predator an animal that hunts or kills other animals for food. Owls and lynx are examples of predators.

prey an animal that is hunted and killed for food. The snowshoe rabbit is the lynx's prey.

resin a substance produced by plants that can be clear or cloudy, yellow or brown, and solid or semisolid.

solar radiation the heat and light created by the sun.

species a group of organisms that are genetically similar and can interbreed with one another in nature.

stratification the defining characteristic of mountainous ecosystems. Different ecosystems can be found at different strata, or levels, of elevation. By moving up or down a mountainside, you pass from one ecosystem to another.

stratum level of elevation.

subalpine existing below alpine elevations.

succession the process by which a first set of trees in a forest is gradually replaced by another set of trees.

succulents a group of plants specially adapted to a dry climate; many are able to store water in their leaves or stems.

tree line the boundary separating tundra from subalpine forest. Above the tree line, trees cannot grow due to poor soil and extreme weather conditions.

windfall a portion of a forest knocked over by a violent wind. Although this means death to the fallen trees, once down, they become home and food for numerous insects and small animals.

Further Exploration

Books

Burns, Diane L. *Rocky Mountain Seasons*. New York: Macmillan, 1993.

Jennings, Terry J. *Mountains*. Parsippany, NJ: Silver Burdett Press, 1998.

Petersen, David. *Rocky Mountain National Park*. Chicago: Childrens Press, 1993.

Rotter, Charles. *Mountains*. Mankato, MN: Creative Education, 1993.

On the Internet

http://www.nps.gov The National Park Service homepage on the Internet.

http://www.sierraclub.com Homepage for the Sierra Club, a nonprofit, member-supported public interest organization that promotes conservation of the natural environment.

Organizations

Glacier National Park
P. O. Box 128,
West Glacier, MT 59936
(406) 888-7800

Grand Teton National Park
P. O. Drawer 170,
Moose, WY 83012;
(307) 739-3300

Rocky Mountain National Park
Estes Park, CO 80517
(970) 586-1206

Yellowstone National Park
P. O. Box 168,
Yellowstone National Park, WY 82190-0168
(307) 344-7381

Index

Page numbers for illustrations are in **boldface**.